I know that throughout my life
wherever I am
I will always
remember so well
and cherish our friendship
as one of the best
I have ever known

— Susan Polis Schutz

Library of Congress Catalog Card Number: 98-16823
ISBN: 0-88396-467-8

ACKNOWLEDGMENTS appear on page 48.

Certain trademarks are used under license.
BLUE MOUNTAIN PRESS is registered in U.S. Patent and Trademark Office.

Printed in the United States of America.
Tenth Printing: 2005

 This book is printed on recycled paper.

This book is printed on fine quality, laid embossed, 80 lb. paper. This paper has been specially
produced to be acid free (neutral pH) and contains no groundwood or unbleached pulp. It
conforms with all the requirements of the American National Standards Institute, Inc., so as to
ensure that this book will last and be enjoyed by future generations.

Library of Congress Cataloging-in-Publication Data

You're just like a sister to me : poems celebrating the special
    friendships that women share / edited by Patricia Wayant.
        p.   cm.
    ISBN 0-88396-467-8 (alk. paper)
    1. Friendship--Poetry. 2. Female friendship--Poetry. 3. American
poetry--Women authors. 4. Women--Poetry. I. Wayant, Patricia,
1953-   .
PS595.F75Y69 1998
811.008'0353--dc21   98-16823
                                                  CIP

Blue Mountain Arts, Inc.

P.O. Box 4549, Boulder, Colorado 80306

You're Just like a Sister to Me

Poems celebrating the special friendships
that women share

Edited by
Patricia Wayant

Blue Mountain Press™
Boulder, Colorado

You're Just like a Sister to Me

The best kind of friendships are the lasting, warm and wonderful kind that you and I have always shared.

Friendships like ours are the kind where the caring never goes away, the understanding is deep and sweet and sincere, and the two friends are so near in their hearts that they'll stay close forever.

I really cherish having you for a friend. You're the very best kind there is, and it's a privilege to know you as well as I do. But there's something more I need to tell you: you and I have a trust, an honesty, and a history together that makes me think of you as so much more than a friend. You're someone who is at the center of the circle of my life. Someone essential to me.

And I know you'll always stay that way, because when a friend is as close as you are, they're just like family. I can barely even begin to tell you how much you touch my soul, raise my hopes, and inspire my smiles. Maybe the best way to convey it is to lovingly try and say that you've always been and you always will be

...just like a sister to me.

— Emilia Larson

Friends Are the Most Special People in Life

Friends are cherished people
whom we carry in our hearts
wherever we go in life.
We may spend a lot of time
together,
getting to know each other
and sharing each other's life,
then have to move on
to other places.
But no matter where we go,
we always remember
the wonderful people
who touched our lives
and who loved us and helped us
learn more about ourselves.
We always remember the people who stayed by us
when we had to face difficult times,
and with whom we felt safe enough
to reveal our true selves.
Friends are the unforgettable people
we dreamed and planned
great futures with,
who accepted us as we were
and encouraged us to become
all that we wanted to be.

My friend,
no matter where we go in life
or how far apart we are,
you will always be close to me,
and I will always be your friend.

— Donna Levine

Our Friendship Is Very Important to Me

From the first day we met,
   I knew that I could trust you.
I've shared with you my
secret hopes and dreams,
   and you've listened while
   understanding and encouraging me
   to pursue them.
Whenever I've needed you,
you've never been far away,
   comforting me through the bad times
   and laughing with me through the good.
You've always given me good advice,
   trying to help me become
   the best I could be.
Whenever I've felt bad about myself,
   you've always managed to point out
   the qualities you like about me,
   making me feel a little more optimistic.
I've been myself around you
and you've accepted me,
   loving me even for my imperfections.
As our friendship continues to grow,
I want you to remember that
you really are
a very important part of my life.

— Caroline E. Bryant

You're My "Real" Sister

Even though God didn't give us
the same mother and father,
you're my real sister because of
the way you are to me.

You are honest with me; you
trust me and you care about my
welfare. You allow me to know
your weaknesses and trust me to
understand them.

You help me by being interested
in what I am saying and going
through, and you think of those
things when I am not around in
an effort to find answers to
things you know I question.

You allow me to do things for you,
to care for you, and to influence you.
You sense when I need help and
understanding and approval. You
allow me to know things that are
happening in your life, so that
I can try to be those things to you
that you are to me.

You allow me to progress
independently, as I do with you.
You're there, always there. You're my
friend. You don't give up on me
when I disappoint you. Thank you
for that, most of all.

No, we don't have the same mother
and father, but our souls are "akin."
You are my real sister, and our
"kinship" is standing the tests of
time and change.

— Donna Fargo

I Want to Thank You for the Friendship We Share

It's hard to express how much
you have come to mean to me.
You are a dear and special friend
who brightens many of my days.
No matter how bad things get
   in your own life,
you always have time to listen
   and care about
what's going on in mine.
When things get tough,
you help me see the humor in them.
Sharing laughter with you
is one of my favorite things to do,
and your smile often gives me
a much-needed lift.
You have a way about you
that reaches beyond yourself
to embrace the world around you.
Your gentle ways and thoughtfulness
make wherever you are
a comfortable place to be.
Sometimes I wonder if you realize
   your importance
and the positive difference you make
in the lives you touch.
So I wanted to take this opportunity
to remind you of this
and let you know that I'm grateful
to have you as my special friend.

— Barbara Cage

I Appreciate You So Much!

A real friend says,
  "I'll be there for you..."
    and is.
A real friend says,
  "I care about you..."
    and does.
A real friend says,
  "You are important to me..."
    and means it.
A real friend says,
  "Call me when you need me..."
    and answers when you do.
A real friend says,
  "If you need anything,
    let me know..."
      and gives.

By your actions, I know
  that you're a real friend.
Thank you for being there
  for me.

— Doreen Stewart

You Have a Friend in Me Forever

There are certain kinds of friends
who can easily discuss all things,
who feel so utterly comfortable
    with each other,
see one another's inner soul,
and keep faith when things
    go wrong.

For friends like these,
the length of time
they've been together
   is unimportant in determining
     how well they know one another,
and distance means nothing,
   for true friendship has
     no boundaries.

If we should ever grow apart
   in time or distance —
     today, tomorrow,
       or in the days ahead —
our friendship will still be embedded
   in my mind,
     my heart,
       and my soul.
Regardless of where you are,
   know that you have a friend
     in me...
       forever.

— M. Maxine Largman

I Will Always Admire You
as a Woman and as a Friend

You are a woman who
knows what she wants to do
and does it
A woman who
is not afraid to
speak out for what she believes
A woman who
is kind and good and giving
A woman who
sets high goals for herself
and achieves them
A woman who
is beautiful on the outside
and the inside
A woman who
understands herself and
is in complete charge of her life
A woman who
is intelligent and sensitive
strong and able
A woman who
gives so much to her friends
to her family
to everyone

You are a remarkable woman
who is loved by so many people
whose lives you have touched
including mine

— Susan Polis Schutz

You're Everything
a Sister Is!

Sisters care about each other,
  just like we do.

They share the good times
    and the bad,
and they listen without judging
    one another.
They understand one another;
they know when to offer advice,
    and when to listen quietly.

Sisters laugh over things
    only they see the humor in,
and they share each other's
    hurts and troubles,
just like we do.

All I know is that nothing
    could make you
any more special or loved
    than you already are —
because you, my friend,
    are like a sister to me.

— Barbara Cage

You're a Friend Who Knows the True Meaning of Giving

You have touched my life
and my world in a way that
few others have ever done,
and I know I will never be the same.
You have brightened my life
with the gifts of your laughter and joy,
and the comfort of knowing someone cares.
You have stood strong for me
when the rest of the world
seemed not to care.
You have been my true friend
when I had very little friendship
to give back.
You have taken the time to listen
when I needed to talk,
and to hug me when I cried.

You have been my best friend at a time
when I needed one so desperately,
and you have given me courage at a time
when I was lonely and afraid.
I am deeply thankful for all of this,
and for you.

I have received so much from you,
and I hope I can repay it all someday,
for I will always remember
and be thankful for what you
have given me.
You have given me yourself,
the very best gift of all.
You are a friend who knows,
more than anyone I know,
the true meaning of giving.

— Donna Taylor

A Woman Needs a Friend...

To let us bare our souls.
To allow us to free the emotions,
secrets, fantasies, and dreams
that are sometimes beyond the
comprehension of
other people in our lives.
To release our frustrations to,
and whose frustrations
we can help relieve.
To laugh, cry, rejoice,
and share with.
To just be there.

As women, we are not
always strong,
but together we can make it.
True friendship is an
important piece of being a woman.
It helps to know that we have
a place to go where there is
a smile and an ear when needed.
It helps to know we have
friends.

— Susan M. Catalano

You are the one person who shares
   my deepest thoughts
And loves me in spite of them.
You counsel me when my heart is broken and
Stand by me when I'm mistreated.
You rally behind me in my good decisions and
Are there to help me through
   the consequences of the bad ones.
Whom else can I call at any hour
   of the day or night?
Who else accepts and understands all of me?
Not many people are as blessed as I am
With someone like you in their lives.

I don't know why the heavens decided to give me
   the wonderful gift of you as my friend,
But I'm grateful.
Although our paths may lead us in
   different directions,
I know I can always count on you.
No matter what comes along, good or bad,
   you'll be there;
Knowing this brings me great comfort and security.
I hope you know in your heart that
I am that same sort of friend to you.
Our secrets are safe
   and our hearts are protected
Because of the love between us...
Two special friends.

— Pamela Monroe

You're the Sister
I Never Had

For whatever reason,
you came into my life halfway
through its journey.
We didn't have all those yesterdays
of being little girls together.
We didn't share the same
mother and father,
or help each other blow out
our birthday candles.
There weren't any days of playing
hopscotch or tag,
of staying up nights giggling
and planning our futures.
We never experienced the gift of love
that sisters share,
    until now.
I have been so lucky in having had
a life filled with many friends,
but none of them knows my heart
and my spirit as you do.
You have given me something very special,
a gift I never knew I had missed,
and which now
I can't imagine being without...

    the gift of a sister's love.

— Joan Benicken

With You, Any Day
Is a Good Day
for Talking

Keep the coffee warm.
It's a good day for talking.
You share a secret
and I'll share one, too.
I have dozens.
I've been saving them
for you to hear.
Our lives keep us
too far apart for too long
these days.
There are children and husbands
to be nurtured and loved
and mountains of laundry
to be caught up with
before we care for ourselves,
for our friendship.
It's always there, though,
a strong, silent heartbeat
hidden in our routines.
So I'll bring the coffee cake —
or maybe you'd like danish —
and you keep the coffee warm.
It's a good day for talking.

— Laurie Creasy

We've been friends through
   a million things —
in our worst moments
when everything seemed horrible,
and on our best days
when every moment was beautiful.

We've shared all of our thoughts,
   our dreams, and our hearts.
We've kept each other's secrets
   and sworn to be faithful.

We've spent time revealing
   the deepest part of our feelings,
and encouraged each other
   when one of us was insecure.

We've been each other's strength
   during the saddest moments
and shared each other's dreams
   through every change or discouragement.

We've been the best of friends,
   known each other better
   than anyone else,
and accepted each other.

We've shared a lot through the years,
   and I have to tell you
that I love you, my dear friend,
   and I will until the end.

If you ever need a friend...
   please know you can count on me!

— Regina Hill

Sister of My Heart

You are the sister of my heart,
   not born of the same parents,
But born of the same sensibilities,
Emotions, desires, dreams —
Raised in different places
   with different beliefs,
But yet so much alike in thought.
Our hearts and minds draw us yet closer
   to each other.

Share with me your secrets,
   your fantasies, your passions,
And I will share mine with you,
Ever trustful, confident that my secrets,
My deepest musings, are forever safe,
   never to be recounted,
Locked away in your mind,
Where only you and I hold the key,
   the key to my soul.

We are lifelines to one another,
   clinging precariously to the thread
That protects us from the cruelties of reality.
Reach out to me, I will catch you.
I will be with you when you need me —
Ever cognizant that you are my safety net,
   my ballast against the storm.

How can I ever repay you, my friend,
For all the many hours you listened
   to my words, my thoughts?
You were my ally in the ravages of war,
A place I could go to where I knew
   I would be safe from reproach,
Comfortable in the warmth of your friendship.
Thank you, my friend.

— Margie Spickler

Ours Is a Friendship
like No Other...

Sometimes a person is blessed with meeting someone
Who touches their life in a way
That no one else has,
In a way that cannot be explained,
For it is a mutual linking of two hearts,
A bonding of friendship like no other.
You know it is something special
Right from the start,
Even if you have only known the person
For a short time.
But in that time, the foundation
Of a true and lasting friendship
Has already been laid.

A true and lasting friendship
Is built on trust and openness
And understanding.
It is not selfish or demanding and does not
Require you to be someone that you are not.
Rather, it is a friendship
That gives unconditionally
And allows the freedom to express yourself
With no expectations to be anyone different.
It is giving and loving and loyal
And welcomes the sharing of both
Good and bad times with each other.
It brings happiness in thinking of
The other person and
Joy in the time that is spent together.
The warm embraces shared
Have a way of saying everything
That cannot be put into words,
Those things that can be spoken
Only from the heart.

I have been blessed that God put
Such a special person in my life...
Someone in whose confidence I've trusted
And whose friendship and companionship
I've grown to value and treasure.
Thank you for being such a rare individual;
Thank you for our very special friendship.

— Kathleen L. Biela

I Don't Know
What I Would Do
Without You

We both know that life
can be hard sometimes...
We get so caught up in business
and family and children, and
worrying about all those little
things that somehow never
quite get done...
I sometimes wonder
what I'd do if I didn't have you
to remind me of what's most important.

You're a great friend...
You're there to lean on when I'm hurt,
to laugh with (we do a lot of that),
to give me that little kick
when I need a boost,
and to offer me direction
when my life gets a little out of focus.
What would I do without our
endless phone conversations
or our "ladies nights out"?
We always have a good time;
you add something to my life
that was never really there before.
You're the best, and for that
and everything else...
thanks.

— Julia Escobar

As Friends, We've Traveled So Far Together

We've grown up together.
It's hard for me to believe sometimes
that so many years have come and gone.
Photographs of little girls
framed in glass
are a reminder of days gone by
    and memories made.
But today, we are women,
and the daydreams we shared
as little girls in the summer sun
    have become realities.
"Crushes" have become commitments,
and wonder has turned to knowledge.

It amazes me —
how far we've traveled
and how many crossroads
    we've come to together.
But no matter what
    our lives bring us
or how many miles spread
    between us,
we will always be
    those little girls
in our yesterdays
    and in our hearts.

— Megan McKeon

You Could Never Be Replaced in My Life

I wonder if you know that.
Sometimes, you are
the only person in the world
whom I can discuss
a specific problem with.
You know just what to say
to make things okay
when times are tough.
You know just what to do
    to make me smile
and when to make me laugh.
You know when I need
    to cry or complain,
and you listen without
    judging me.
You accept me as I am;
you encourage and support me.
No one else has shared
what we have together —
the laughter or tears,
the secrets and dreams.
I have other friends
    and loved ones,
and each person is special
    in their own way.
But no one could ever take
    your place in my life,
and I just want to be sure
    that you know.

— Barbara Cage

Friendship

Each of us has a hidden place
Somewhere deep within ourselves —
A place where we go to get away
To think things through,
To be alone, to be ourselves.

This unique place, where we
    confront our deepest feelings,
Becomes a storehouse of all our hopes,
All our needs, all our dreams,
And even our unspoken fears.
It encompasses the essence of who we are
And what we want to be.

But now and then, whether by
    chance or design,
Someone discovers a way into this place
We thought was ours alone.
And we allow that person to see,
    to feel, to share
All the reason, all the uncertainty,
And all the emotion we've
    stored up there.

That person adds new perspective
    to our hidden realm,
Then quietly settles down in her
    own corner
Of our special place,
Where a bit of her will
    stay forever.

And we call that person a friend.

— Carol Elaine Faivre-Scott

A Friend...

Someone who is concerned with everything you do ❧ someone to call upon during good and bad times ❧ someone who understands whatever you do ❧ someone who tells you the truth about yourself ❧ someone who knows what you are going through at all times ❧ someone who does not compete with you ❧ someone who is genuinely happy for you when things go well ❧ someone who tries to cheer you up when things don't go well ❧ someone who is an extension of yourself without which you are not complete ❧

— Susan Polis Schutz

Let Me Tell You About My Greatest Friend...

She listens like no one else can.
She's supportive, caring,
    and concerned —
and it always shows.
She stands beside me, come what may,
through good or bad times.
There's no doubt about her loyalty;
each time I've needed
    great encouragement
and someone to depend on,
she has given me all those reasons
    to go on.
She understands me
    like no one else on earth.
Sometimes, it's just as if
    she reads my heart
and responds from her own.

I feel so close to her because
she has made it easy to do so;
she gives me the rarest kind
    of closeness
in the form of a friendship
I can always count on.

I hope these words will find
    their way into her heart
with extra-special meaning,
just to let her know
our friendship works both ways —
that just as she is always
here for me,
I always am for her.
I feel so lucky, for I have found
the greatest friend of all.

— Barbara J. Hall

Best Friends
Are Forever

Best friends always remember so well
all the things they did together
all the subjects they discussed
all the mistakes they made
all the fun they had

Best friends always remember
how their friendship
was such a stabilizing force
during confusing times
in their lives

Best friends may have different lifestyles
live in different places
and interact with different people
but no matter how much
their lives may change
their friendship remains the same

I know that throughout my life
wherever I am
I will always
remember so well
and cherish our friendship
as one of the best
I have ever known

— Susan Polis Schutz

You Are Amazing

So often, I have looked
into your eyes
and been amazed at
how much of myself
I see in you.
So often, I have noticed
how easily a smile comes
whenever you are around
and how safe my heart feels
when it's within the sound
of your voice.

It is not often
that people connect
the way that we have.
It is not often
that you find a friend
who shares and knows
what's in your heart
and who believes
in your dreams
even when you don't.

It is not often
that you find a friend
who is honest enough
to disagree,
humble enough to say,
"I'm sorry,"
and loving enough
to forgive.
So often, I have looked
into your eyes
and been amazed
at how lucky I am
to have you
as my friend.

— Tracia Gloudemans

Friends like You Are Forever

Sometimes in life,
you find a special friend:
someone who changes your life
by being a part of it.
Someone who makes you laugh
until you can't stop;
someone who makes you believe
that there really is
good in the world.
Someone who convinces you
that there is an unlocked door
just waiting for you to open it.
This is forever friendship.

When you're down,
and the world seems dark and empty,
your forever friend lifts you up in spirit
and makes that dark and empty world
suddenly seem bright and full.
Your forever friend gets you through
the hard times, the sad times,
and the confused times.
If you turn and walk away,
your forever friend follows.
If you lose your way,
your forever friend guides you
and cheers you on.
Your forever friend holds your hand
and tells you that
everything is going to be okay.
And if you find such a friend,
you feel happy and complete,
because you need not worry.
You have a forever friend for life,
and forever has no end.

— Laurieann Kelly

You Have Touched
My Life

You know when someone special
touches your life...
  They always know just the right
    thing to say or do;
  They can make you feel better
    just by being near;
  They listen with an open heart
    and understand;
  They laugh with you when you're happy;
  They share your tears when you're sad;
  They are there beside you
    whenever you feel alone;
  They extend their hand when
    you need support;
  They are proud of all that
    you accomplish;
  They love you just because you're you.

You know when someone special
    touches your life...
And my life was touched
    the day that I met you.

— Geri Danks

We Are Sisters of the Heart

You and I were born miles apart,
but our lives have taken the same roads.
We have shared secrets, dreams,
and hopes.
We have laughed and cried at the
same things.
We have experienced the joy of finding
pieces of ourselves in each other.
Though we are not related by birth,
we are related by soul.
We are sisters of the heart.

— Sarah Alexander

You Are a
Very Good Friend

We have all had many friends
throughout our lives,
but only a few of them
we would call good friends.

That's because being a good friend
involves time
and understanding
and love,
which can be difficult to share with another.
When I think of my good friends,
I always think about you,
because that is what you have been to me.
You have taken the time
to be there when I needed you,
and you have listened to me
when my life was changing.
You have always cared enough
to try to understand my feelings
and help me to understand myself.
And, most important,
your consideration and honesty
have shown me that your friendship is true...
symbolizing a very special kind of love
that only a few friends
ever share with one another.
Thank you for being such
a good friend to me,
and for all the joys we have known
together.

— Laura Medley

It Means So Much to Me to Have You as a Friend

Sometimes life moves by so quickly,
and I just can't seem to keep track
   of the days,
let alone steal a few minutes to
tell you what it means to me
   to be your friend.

As friends, we've developed
a wonderful trust between us.
We each know that the other is
always just a phone call away
and that if something is needed
we only have to ask.

I like the way our personalities
blend so neatly together
and how you can always make me smile.
It's nice to know that someone out there
understands who I am.

That's why I need you to know
that you're appreciated
and admired and respected
and honestly loved.
"Friend" is one of the most beautiful
   words I know...
Thank you for giving it so much meaning.

— Jennifer Kristin Ellis

You'll Always Be
like Family to Me

You're the friend who's been so good to me,
the one I tell my troubles to,
the one who listens carefully
and always understands.

You're the friend I feel closest to.
There have been so many times when
I gave you all my fears and hurts,
and each time you gave back a heart
filled with love and concern,
a shoulder to rest my worries upon,
and a tranquility found nowhere else on earth.

You're the friend who means so much to me,
the one I'm thinking of right now,
the one who feels like family in my heart.
And more than anything else,
I want you to know that I'm here for you,
just as you've always been for me...

Because you're like a sister to me.

— Barbara J. Hall

ACKNOWLEDGMENTS

The following is a partial list of authors whom the publisher especially wishes to thank for permission to reprint their works.

PrimaDonna Entertainment Corp. for "You're My 'Real' Sister," by Donna Fargo. Copyright © 1998 by PrimaDonna Entertainment Corp. All rights reserved.

Barbara Cage for "I Want to Thank You for the Friendship We Share" and "You're Everything a Sister Is!" Copyright © 1998 by Barbara Cage. All rights reserved.

Susan M. Catalano for "A Woman Needs a Friend...." Copyright © 1998 by Susan M. Catalano. All rights reserved.

Pamela Monroe for "You are the one person who shares...." Copyright © 1998 by Pamela Monroe. All rights reserved.

Laurie Creasy for "With You, Any Day Is a Good Day For Talking." Copyright © 1998 by Laurie Creasy. All rights reserved.

Margie Spickler for "Sister of My Heart." Copyright © 1998 by Margie Spickler. All rights reserved.

Kathleen Biela for "Ours Is a Friendship like No Other." Copyright © 1998 by Kathleen Biela. All rights reserved.

Julia Escobar for "I Don't Know What I Would Do Without You." Copyright © 1998 by Julia Escobar. All rights reserved.

Megan McKeon for "As Friends, We've Traveled So Far Together." Copyright © 1998 by Megan McKeon. All rights reserved.

Carol Elaine Faivre-Scott for "Friendship." Copyright © 1998 by Carol Elaine Faivre-Scott. All rights reserved.

Barbara J. Hall for "Let Me Tell You About My Greatest Friend...." Copyright © 1998 by Barbara J. Hall. All rights reserved.

Tracia Gloudemans for "You Are Amazing." Copyright © 1998 by Tracia Gloudemans. All rights reserved.

Sarah Alexander for "We Are Sisters of the Heart." Copyright © 1998 by Sarah Alexander. All rights reserved.

A careful effort has been made to trace the ownership of poems used in this anthology in order to obtain permission to reprint copyrighted materials and give proper credit to the copyright owners. If any error or omission has occurred, it is completely inadvertent, and we would like to make corrections in future editions provided that written notification is made to the publisher:

BLUE MOUNTAIN ARTS, INC., P.O. Box 4549, Boulder, Colorado 80306.